Under Thy Wings I Will Trust Workbook

Helping you to work your story of Healing, Deliverance and Restoration.

Zolisha L. Ware

Copyright © 2019 by Zolisha L. Ware

All rights reserved. No part of this publication may be reproduced by any means, graphics, electronic, or mechanical, including photocopying, recording, taping, or by any information storage retrieval system without the written permission of the publisher except in the case of brief quotations embodied in critical articles and reviews.

Zolisha L. Ware/Rejoice Essential Publishing
PO BOX 512
Effingham, SC 29541
www.republishing.org

Unless otherwise indicated, scripture is taken from the King James Version.

Scripture quotations marked (NLT) are taken from the Holy Bible, New Living Translation, copyright ©1996, 2004, 2015 by Tyndale House Foundation. Used by permission of Tyndale House Publishers, Inc., Carol Stream, Illinois 60188. All rights reserved.

Scripture quotations marked (ESV) are taken from the Holy Bible, English Standard Version® (ESV®) Copyright © 2001 by Crossway, a publishing ministry of Good News Publishers. All rights reserved.

Under Thy Wings, I Will Trust Workbook/ Zolisha L. Ware

ISBN-10: 1-946756-66-0
ISBN-13: 978-1-946756-66-4

Dedication

To my Lord and Savior, who delivered me out of the hands of the enemy: You healed and restored me for Your namesake so that I may be of some use for the Kingdom. In You, I live and have my being. I am eternally grateful for my second chance to complete all that I have been called to do. For Your love covered and kept me until I was able to cover another.

I also dedicate this workbook to all those who have invested in their learning and are eager to prune themselves for our Savior's namesake. May the goodness and mercy of our God follow you all the days of your life.

Table of Contents

ACKNOWLEDGMENT..ix

PREFACE...xi

INTRODUCTION...1

LESSON 1:   Life Happens..3

LESSON 2:   I'm Grown..9

LESSON 3:   Party Time..15

LESSON 4:   I Do...21

LESSON 5:   Life to Christ...27

LESSON 6:   The Blood of Jesus....................................33

LESSON 7:   Broken Marriage..39

LESSON 8:   Marriage Sanctification..........................46

LESSON 9:   Overcomer...52

LESSON 10:   Come Forth..58

LESSON 11:   Words of Expression................................64

CLOSING REMARKS..66

ABOUT THE AUTHOR..67

WORKS CITED...70

Acknowledgments

I acknowledge my Lord and Savior Jesus Christ who healed me, delivered me and called me forth for His glorious service. Timothy 3:16 says, "All scripture given by inspiration of God and is profitable for doctrine, for reproof, for correction, for instruction in righteousness." I also acknowledge the Lord for this workbook who gave me the design that it may instruct, correct and edify the body of Christ that we all would be used for the service of our Lord and Savior.

Preface

Deliverance is a process of renewal that continues whether you are a babe in Christ or a mature believer. The Bible says that deliverance is the children's bread (Matthew 15:26). We all know that bread is something we need daily to survive. Thus, deliverance is just as important for us to be strong and powerful in Christ. The Word says to be strong in the Lord in the power of His might (Ephesians 6:10). Deliverance never stops. If you are in this body, you will need God's continued edification until our Lord and Savior return. This book was birth out of that understanding received while in prayer.

Before we get started, please take some time to understand what the word STRONGHOLD means. A stronghold is defined as a place dominated by a particular group or marked by a particular characteristic (2019 Merriam-Webster, Stronghold, 2019). Many believers are stuck because of strongholds or faulty character traits within their lives. Some are noticeable, and others hidden. As believers, our job is to examine ourselves daily to be found within our faith. Examining ourselves means to open your heart as you meditate on God's Word. Then you'll be able to pull down everything that exalts itself within you that is not a character trait of Jesus Christ. A walk with Christ is a consistent process, that must be endured to prepare us for Christ's return. I implore you to open your heart in this study and allow God to show you the hidden things. That way, you may grow stronger to help yourself and be able to minister to another.

STRONGHOLDS

For though we walk in the flesh, we do not war after the flesh: (For the weapons of our warfare are not carnal, but mighty through God to the pulling down of strongholds:) casting down imaginations, and every high thing that exalted itself against the knowledge of God, and bringing into captivity every thought to the obedience of Christ. --2 Corinthians 10:3-5

1. What walls does the enemy have you bound by?

_____
_____
_____
_____
_____
_____
_____
_____
_____
_____
_____

2. Are you ready to use the hammer that breaks the rock in pieces (Jeremiah 23:29)?

_____
_____
_____
_____
_____
_____
_____
_____
_____
_____
_____

3. Have you prepared yourself to be delivered from every stronghold in your life?

_____
_____
_____
_____
_____
_____
_____

4. What strongholds are you aware of in your life?

5. Final Thoughts:

_____

_____

_____

_____

_____

_____

_____

_____

_____

_____

_____

Dear Heavenly Father,

I pray that every person that reads this book be free from anything that's within them and creating limits within their life. Lord, we know that nothing is impossible with You unto those who please You. Thus, we understand our limitations come from the enemy who blocks us with the cares of this life, emotions, and generations curses. Lord, I ask You to forgive and uproot any graven images in the lives of the readers currently or in past generations that they may see You like never before. Lord, I ask You to release fresh winds upon them that they will feel you're passing through, which will bring healing, deliverance, and freedom. God, You are the finisher of our faith. Help them to know You better than ever. Lord, help every reader to want You more than ever. Lord, allow them to dwell with You like never before, and to see You in their everyday lives, every second of the day. Lord, I love You and magnify You. Thank You for all You do in the seen and unseen things. I ask all these things in Your son Jesus' name. Amen.

Introduction

As sure as we live, life is going to happen. Some are in survival mode and merely existing. The modern church not only has to teach believers to have a relationship with Christ, but they have the responsibility to teach new converts how to come out of survival mode and to live. The Bible teaches us, according to John 10:10 (ESV), "The thief comes only to steal and kill and destroy. I came that they may have life and have it abundantly." Jesus came to bring new life by shaping the believer to edify, comfort, and build the Kingdom of God.

Many people are trapped living in survival mode bound by hardship without Christ; this will ultimately be an unmerciful cycle. If the delivering power of Jesus Christ does not save them, it creates a life of shame, heartache, and corruption that will follow them all the days of their life, which conceptualizes my life. Before Christ, I was so full of insecurities, hatred, rejection, pride, and envy. I didn't like people because "people hurt other people." God taught me that it wasn't the people, but this corrupt world system that shapes the minds of people, causing them to inflict pain on those around them if they are not healed.

WORKBOOK DIRECTION

Read each supporting paragraph. Then review each stronghold. Go to each Scripture supplied and read it. Be sure to read every correlating Scripture you will find as you study. You can use online study tools or any study Bible. Then come back and write your initial thoughts on that topic. Secondly, complete a self-evaluation and answer the following question. Are you struggling with that stronghold currently or did you struggle in the past with that issue? How did you overcome the stronghold? How do you continually stay free of the stronghold? Next, after meditating on the stronghold, ask yourself, did God reveal anything to you concerning the topic as a whole? Finally, with all the information learned, how will you apply the information that it may be of some use to those around you struggling from these issues? I've also listed some extra questions to think about under many of the listed topics. Please use the space provided within the workbook to track your answers for future reflection.

LESSON 1

Life Happens

Family systems have been dismantled from the original plan of God affecting households with one husband and one wife. Sex outside of marriage has devastating consequences. One of the consequences is that individuals find themselves with no support, which creates life struggles that turn into generational curses that continue over many generations. This curse not only continues the cycle of having children out of marriage, but also creates poverty-stricken generations bound by brokenness, bitterness, envy, and strife. That consequence then leads those who are stuck within cycles, which ultimately leads to finding avenues for relief that only create more evil patterns leading only to death. These corrupt seeds produce corrupt fruit that will continue without someone bringing the life of Christ into the picture.

STRONGHOLDS

1. Wicked Communication (1 Corinthians 15:33)
Be not deceived: evil communications corrupt good manners.
a.   Do you struggle with wicked communication?
b.   Are you on the receiving or sending end of the communication?

c. What does God's Word say about wicked communication?

_____
_____
_____
_____
_____
_____
_____
_____
_____
_____
_____

2. Rejection (Psalms 27:10 NLT)
When my father and my mother forsake me, then the LORD will take me up.
a. Do you suffer from rejection?
b. How do you discard the emotions once you have been rejected?
c. What practices are in place to keep you from rejecting those around you?

_____
_____
_____
_____

3. Identity (Romans 6:6; 1 Peter 2:9)
Knowing this, that our old man is crucified with him, that the body of sin might be destroyed, that henceforth we should not serve sin. But ye are a chosen generation, a royal priesthood, a holy nation, a peculiar people; that ye should shew forth the praises of him who hath called you out of darkness into his marvelous light.

a. What identity have you chosen?
b. Do you know who you truly are?
c. What is your purpose?
d. How will your identity serve others?

4. Fornication (1 Thessalonians 4:3-4)

For this is the will of God, even your sanctification, that ye should abstain from fornication: That every one of you should know how to possess his vessel in sanctification and honor;

a.   Is your body subjected to the Lord in every way?
b.   Have you allowed your fleshy needs to lead you?

5. Generational Curses (Exodus 20:5; 34:7; Numbers 14:18; Deuteronomy 5:9)

The Bible mentions "generational curses" in several places (Exodus 20:5; 34:7; Numbers 14:18; Deuteronomy 5:9). God warns that He is a jealous

God, punishing the children for the sin of the fathers to the third and fourth generation of those who hate Him.

a. What cycles are in your life that seems to repeat?
b. Have you asked God to reveal where they come from?
c. Have you asked forgiveness for you and all past generations?

_____
_____
_____
_____
_____
_____
_____
_____
_____
_____
_____

6. Final Thoughts:
_____
_____
_____
_____
_____
_____

LESSON 2

Growing Pains

With the world moving fast, many families are being lost. Today, most households need a two-household income to maintain to make it. Thus, creating a gap that causes many families to count on older children to help support working parents. However, in so doing, children suffer, which may be unintentional but because there are no other choices for a financially struggling family. Ultimately, this causes the oldest child to be responsible for the younger ones. Once the oldest child has been put into an adult role, many issues can arise. Parents and those supporting the family must watch the child ensuring that they are still allowed to partake in age-appropriate activities.

Ephesians 6:4 states, "Fathers, do not provoke your children to anger, but bring them up in the discipline and instruction of the Lord." Without discipline, children can become wild and untamed. If not caught in time, this can turn into strongholds that will continue within the child's life until they are delivered. Add on a child that is raised outside of the Christian beliefs, and now you have a complex life with open doors to strongholds, false principles, and broken understanding of life.

That child can become hazardous not only to themselves but to all who encounter them.

STRONGHOLDs

1. Emotional Healing (Proverbs 29:11)
A fool gives full vent to his spirit, but a wise man quietly holds it back.
a.   Are your emotions in control of you, or are you in control of your emotions?
b.   Have you given all your desires over to the Lord?
c.   Are you on the right path, or are you turned over to the enemy?

_____
_____
_____
_____
_____
_____
_____
_____
_____
_____
_____

2. Mental Stumbling Blocks (Jerimiah 17:14)
Heal me, O Lord, and I will be healed; save me, and I will be saved, for you are the one I praise."

a. Are you carrying the mind of Christ?
b. Have you been turned over to your reprobate mind?

_____
_____
_____
_____
_____
_____
_____
_____
_____
_____
_____

3. Lust of the Flesh (Psalms 101:3)
I will not look with approval on anything that is vile. I hate what faithless people do; I will have no part in it.
a. Is your faith in your looks?
b. Is your faith in what others think of you?
c. Is your faith in what God says concerning you?

_____
_____
_____
_____
_____

4. Rejection (1 Peter 2:4)

As you come to him, the living Stone rejected by humans but chosen by God and precious to him.

a. Are you taking on the rejection pushed on you?

b. Are you casting down anything that is not of God?

5. Hopelessness (Psalms 40:2)

He brought me up also out of the pit of hopelessness, out of the miry clay and set my feet upon a rock and straightened my steps.

a. What is your present help?
b. Are you building your faith?
c. Are you allowing faith to guide you?
d. Do you need God to increase your faith?
e. Have you fasted and prayed on the matter?

_____
_____
_____
_____
_____
_____
_____
_____
_____
_____
_____
_____

6. Final Thoughts:

_____
_____
_____
_____

LESSON 3

Party Time

Partying can be a stage of life that can take you years to get over. Why? Because when you thought you were free, you've created a false persona that caused you to mask many of your pains and hurts into false freedom. A great example of this occurred in my life. I was no longer living in my parents' home because I had children early. Thus, I could play house. Not by my parents' choice but by force of the decisions I had made. My mother tried to stop me, but I wanted what I wanted. The more my mother tried to save me, the harder I pushed. My mother allowed me to learn from the school of the hard knocks and boy did I have to learn.

The choices we make can haunt us for most of our life. As a teen or young adult, you can think those choices create the freedom to do whatever your heart desires. However, if those decisions are not based on the Word of God, then you will find yourself bound by the cares of this world with no way of escape. This causes you to make one bad decision after another because you have created a path of destruction that only those on the outside can see. There is a God that can break every chain and set every life straight if we call on Him. God's Word says in 1 Corinthians

10:13 (ESV), "No temptation has overtaken you that is not common to man. God is faithful, and he will not let you be tempted beyond your ability, but with the temptation, He will also provide the way of escape, that you may be able to endure it."

STRONGHOLDS

1. Psychological Distortion (John 8:32)
   And ye shall know the truth, and the truth shall make you free.
   a. Do lies blind you?
   b. Are you truly looking for the truth?

   _____
   _____
   _____
   _____
   _____
   _____
   _____
   _____
   _____
   _____

2. Turmoil (Job 3:17)
   There the wicked ceases from turmoil, and there the weary are at rest.
   a. Are you carrying childhood pains?

b. Have you forgiven those that hurt you?

c. Have you cast those pains unto the Lord?

_____
_____
_____
_____
_____
_____
_____
_____
_____
_____
_____
_____

3. PTSD - Posttraumatic Stress Disorder (Psalms 61:2-3)

From the end of the earth will I cry unto thee, when my heart is overwhelmed: lead me to the rock that is higher than I. For thou hast been a shelter for me, and a strong tower from the enemy.

a. Are you carrying childhood, adolescent, or adult trauma?

b. Have you forgiven those that caused the trauma?

c. Have you given your heart unto the Lord for complete healing?

_____
_____
_____
_____

4. Shame (Genesis 3:7)

He said, "I heard the sound of you in the garden, and I was afraid because I was naked; so, I hid myself."

   a.   Have you laid naked and not ashamed before the Lord?

   b.   Have you allowed Him to heal you entirely, or are you still masking the pain?

5. Covetousness (Ephesians 5:5)

For this ye know, that no whoremonger, nor unclean person, nor covetous man, who is an idolater, hath any inheritance in the kingdom of Christ and of God.

    a. Do you desire someone else's wife or husband?
    b. Do you desire someone else's life?
    c. Do you desire anything above your love of God? Examine all aspects of your physical and mental life.

6. Final Thoughts:

LESSON 4

I Do

Marriage is a sacred covenant created by God. This bond is between a man and a woman designed for procreation. This covenant will allow two to become one, promising a life that would continue the process of worshiping and magnify God while subduing the earth. However, a man and woman whose relationship is not built on God's foundation will struggle with allowing their relationship to be conformed to the things of Christ. They will participate in sexual behaviors that defile the God-ordained order of the things of God. One major thing today that is plaguing this world is fornication and adultery. Everything in this world reflects some form of sexual desire. This generation is about who has the biggest breasts, booty, or who can show the most nakedness. There is nothing left to the imagination, but everything is out in the open. We must make sure we are whole before we take part in a sacred relationship called marriage.

STRONGHOLDS

1. Refused (1 John 1:9)

   If we confess our sins, He is faithful and just and will forgive us our sins and purify us from all unrighteousness.

   a. When is the last time you confessed?
   b. I mean completely confessed your faults unto the Lord?

   _____
   _____
   _____
   _____
   _____
   _____
   _____
   _____
   _____
   _____
   _____
   _____

2. Survival Mode (John 16:33)

   I have said these things to you, that in me you may have peace. In the world, you will have tribulation. But take heart; I have overcome the world.

   a. How often do you cast your troubles unto the Lord?
   b. After casting them upon the Lord, are you picking them back up?

3. Desire (Galatians 5:16)
   So, I say, walk by the Spirit, and you will not gratify the desires of the flesh.
   a. Is your flesh or the Spirit of God leading you?
   b. Have you sought the Lord for the Holy Ghost? It will lead you to all truth.

4. Envy (Titus 3:3)

For we also once were foolish ourselves, disobedient, deceived, enslaved to various lusts and pleasures, spending our life in malice and envy, hateful, hating one another.

    a. Do you have envy in your heart? Do you envy people, places, or things?

    b. Do you desire more?

    c. Are you preparing for the more?

5. Wicked Conversation (Psalms 10:7)

His mouth is full of curses and deceit and oppression; under his tongue is mischief and wickedness.

    a.   Do you talk down to yourself?

    b.   Do you talk down to others?

    c.   Are you seasoning your words with grace?

_____

_____

_____

_____

_____

_____

_____

_____

_____

_____

_____

_____

6. Final Thoughts:

_____

_____

_____

_____

_____

LESSON 5
Life to Christ

When an individual first gives their life to Christ, things are an absolute mess. God must come in and clean the land. Many people look at the land as the city or country they live in, which is true. However, God also looks at our land as our individual lives or as land that needs to be recovered inclusive of our physical bodies. In our lands, we can have unhealthy relationships, which is synonymous with living in the wrong cities, towns, or regions. We could be married to the wrong person or be in abusive relationships that produce physical and emotional abuse. We can be in the wrong careers, educational institution, or church. When we first come to God, He must clean our entire lives, which includes our atmospheres, physical living environment, career or job environment, and every relationship. God must teach us how to make Him our source and everything else in this life is seen as a resource. God must build our lives like His and unroot everything placed by the enemy to destroy us. God is not just doing temporary fixes but everlasting changes that you may one day be able to witness the goodness and mercy of God to the world.

STRONGHOLDS

1. Evil Associations (Psalms 26:4)
   I do not sit with deceitful men, nor will I go with pretenders.
   a. What type of friendships do you have?
   b. Are your relationships one-sided?

   _____
   _____
   _____
   _____
   _____
   _____
   _____
   _____
   _____
   _____
   _____

2. Unforgiveness (John 20:23)
   "If you forgive the sins of any, their sins have been forgiven them; if you retain the sins of any, they have been retained."
   a. Do you have unforgiveness in your heart?
   b. Is that unforgiveness hidden?

   _____
   _____
   _____

3. Pride (1 Samuel 2:3)

Do not multiply your words of pride, let not vain-glory come out of your mouth; For Jehovah is a God of knowledge, and by him actions are weighed.

   a. Are you boastful?
   b. Do you praise God?
   c. Do you praise others in false humility?

4. Strife (Genesis 13:8)

And Abram said unto Lot, let there be no strife, I pray thee, between me and thee, and between my herdsmen and thy herdsmen; for we be brethren.

    a. Are you violent when you become angry?

    b. Are you holding angry in your heart waiting on an opportunity for revenge?

5. Yearning (Isaiah 63:15)

Look down from heaven and see from Your lofty home-holy and beautiful. Where is Your zeal and Your might? Your yearning and your compassion are withheld from me.
   a. Is your desire for God above all other desires in your life?
   b. What is your primary source for all things in your life?

_____
_____
_____
_____
_____
_____
_____
_____
_____
_____
_____
_____

6. Final Thoughts:

_____
_____
_____
_____

LESSON 6

The Blood of Jesus

When new believers come to Christ, God must make them whole. This chapter focuses on the physical portion of healing for new believers. The previous chapter discussed how God heals the land or the surrounding life of believers. Many come to the Lord broken, sick, and confused. The Bible presents countless amounts of healings Jesus did when He was on earth. Today, we hear preached repeatedly, "God is able." No one stands boldly to say, "God can do it right now!" Jesus was a doer. His faith was impeccable not because of uncertainty, but He knew just the smallest faith could birth deliverance for the masses. Believers get caught up in many theological things about Christ, but I have only seen a few stand up to say the words that Jesus gave us full authority to say, "YOUR SINS ARE FORGIVEN TAKE UP YOU BE AND WALK (Luke 5:17-39)." We spend so much time talking about what the people are doing wrong and what the enemy is doing. What about what our God is doing in the earth? He has already told us in His Word that there is nothing new under the sun. Therefore, we know there will always be doubters, those with unbelief, and those who will misuse the gift bestowed on them, which is no different than in Jesus' day.

We need to take more time sharing with others about the goodness of our Lord and wait in expectation for Him to do the rest. None of us have any power; it is God who does it all. Thus, why give any room to the enemy? Why talk of false works? Instead, let our words be seasoned with faith, magnifying our God because we know that He will move when we allow Him too. There is nothing to worry about in this world. Greater is He that is in us than him that is in this world. Thus, let's focus on our passing through while trying to pick as many people up as we can while we wait. We need to be loosing the pure unadulterated Word and works of Christ that all may hear, "Thus saith the Lord," and be free.

STRONGHOLDS

1. Disease (Psalms 107:20)

He sent his Word, and healed them, and delivered them from their destructions.
   a. Are you open to God for healing?
   b. Have you asked Him to heal you, or are you just waiting?
   c. What are you waiting on?
   d. Have you gone to your elders in the church to pray for you?

_____
_____
_____
_____
_____
_____
_____
_____

_____
_____
_____

2. Weakness (1 Corinthians 2:3)

   And I was with you in weakness, and in fear, and in much trembling.

   a. Are you asking the Lord to be your strength?

   b. Are you trying to control the situations that are draining your strength?

_____
_____
_____
_____
_____
_____
_____
_____
_____
_____
_____

3. Doubter (Mark 4:40)

   And he said unto them, Why are ye so fearful? How is it that ye have no faith?

   a. Do you practice having faith daily?

   b. Do you trust God?

4. Grief (1 Samuel 25:31)

That this shall be no grief unto thee, nor offense of heart unto my Lord, either that thou hast shed blood causeless, or that my Lord hath avenged himself: but when the LORD shall have dealt well with my Lord, then remember thine handmaid.
   a. Have you given the pain unto the Lord?
   b. Have you confessed to Him how the situation is affecting you?
   c. Are you honest with yourself where you stand?

5. Blind (Psalms 146:8)

The LORD openeth the eyes of the blind: the LORD raiseth them that are bowed down: the LORD loveth the righteous:
   a. Are you really looking for the Lord?
   b. Is your heart open to truly see Him?

6. Final Thoughts:

LESSON 7

Broken Marriage

When either a man or a woman are saved after marriage, and one spouse is unconverted, there is a process that the couple must go through. God's Word says in 1 Corinthians 7:14, "For the unbelieving husband is sanctified by the wife, and the unbelieving wife is sanctified by the husband: else were our children unclean, but now are they holy." Hence, if they can live together, peaceably in the same home, the wife or husband may stay with their unsaved spouse. Many women don't make it past this stage because they have been brainwashed in believing that once we are saved everything aligns. However, I'm here to tell you that if you really want your marriage, be ready to fight! Everything you thought was bad before gets intensified. You must learn how to set your face like a flint and withstand the wiles of the enemy. God's Word says in Isaiah 50:7, "But the Lord GOD helps me; therefore, I have not been disgraced; therefore, I have set my face like a flint, and I know that I shall not be put to shame." Ephesian 6:11 says, "Put on the whole armor of God, that you may be able to stand against the schemes of the devil." You must be ready to fight in prayer, and by fasting for your spouse. You'll become blind to their sin by focusing on the outcome of winning them to Christ.

Many of us want beautiful marriages, but we don't want the work it takes to have one. Couples who are married outside of God not only have to worry about their salvation. They must bring the marriage under the subjection of the Lord, where both parties agree to follow Christ according to His word. We must apply Ephesians 4:2, "Be completely humble and gentle; be patient, bearing with one another in love." 1 Peter 4:8 says, "Above all, love each other deeply because love covers over a multitude of sins." John 15:12 says, "My command is this: Love each other as I have loved you." Remember on your hardest day that love conquers all. It was love that allowed you to see your wicked way, and it will be love that allows your spouse to see the need for Christ.

STRONGHOLDS

1. Hate (1 John1:6)

If we claim to have fellowship with Him and yet walk in the darkness, we lie and do not live out the truth.

   a. Have you forgiven the person who hurt you or did you just bury the hurt?

   b. Are you ready to dig it up and release the pain unto the Lord?

_____

_____

_____

_____

_____

_____

_____

_____

2. Disobedience (Leviticus 26:14-17)

"But if you will not listen to me and will not do all these commandments, if you spurn my statutes, and if your soul abhors my rules, so that you will not do all my commandments, but break my covenant, then I will do this to you: I will visit you with panic, with wasting disease and fever that consume the eyes and make the heartache. And you shall sow your seed in vain, for your enemies shall eat it. I will set my face against you, and you shall be struck down before your enemies. Those who hate you shall rule over you, and you shall flee when none pursues you."

    a. Have you submitted yourself unto the Lord?

    b. Are you allowing God to lead, or are you leading?

3. Anger (James 1:19-20)

My dear brothers and sisters, take note of this: Everyone should be quick to listen, slow to speak, and slow to become angry because human anger does not produce the righteousness that God desires.

    a. What are your actions when you are angry?
    b. Are you out of control when angry?
    c. What kind of words do you use when angry?
    d. Do they bring life or death?

_____
_____
_____
_____
_____
_____
_____
_____
_____
_____
_____

4. Hostile (Roman 8:6-9)

For to set the mind on the flesh is death, but to set the mind on the Spirit is life and peace. For the mind that is set on the flesh is hostile to God, for it does not submit to God's law; indeed, it cannot. Those who are in the flesh cannot please God. You, however, are not in the flesh but

in the Spirit, if in fact the Spirit of God dwells in you. Anyone who does not have the Spirit of Christ does not belong to him.
   a. What are you focusing on, the situation or the promises of God?
   b. Are you open to correction?
   c. Are you open to forgiveness?

_____
_____
_____
_____
_____
_____
_____
_____
_____
_____
_____
_____

5. Temptation (I Corinthians 10:13)

No temptation has overtaken you except what is common to mankind. And God is faithful; he will not let you be tempted beyond what you can bear. But when you are tempted, he will also provide a way out so that you can endure it.
   a. What do you do when temptation comes?
   b. Are you flee or inviting that temptation into your life?

_____
_____

6. Final Thoughts

LESSON 8

Marriage Sanctification

Once a man and woman become married in Christ, or a couple that was married before Christ, and both parties become saved, the Lord will then sanctify the marriage for use within the Kingdom. That is not to say the Lord can't use one part of the couple if they are saved and the other person is not. However, once a married couple is in Christ, God helps them to become one in Him that they can bring greater works within the Kingdom. Not only can that couple help other newly saved couples, but they teach the individual about their identity in Christ without tearing down, but sharpening each other like a two-edged sword. Marriage is one of the covenants the enemy attacks. I believe he attacks marriage because it exemplifies the very thing in the earth that God promises us. In Genesis, God told the first couple to take dominion and subdue the earth. Thus, when two people come together with greater dominion on earth, there is less room for the enemy. Everywhere the feet of a couple goes that God governs, life is subject to be cultivated, planted, and produce forth a harvest over again until Jesus returns. Not only are they cultivating current lands, but that couple is taking uncultivated territory by force for the Glory of the Lord. Proper sanctification must occur so neither party becomes stagnated or lost during the process.

STRONGHOLDS

1. Disgust (Ecclesiastes 1:2)

    Vanity of vanities, says the preacher, vanity of vanities! All is vanity.

    a. What standard are you holding people in your life? To your standards or the Lord's standards?

    b. Have you been honest about what is happening before you?

    c. Have you prayed to the Lord about your emotions?

    _____
    _____
    _____
    _____
    _____
    _____
    _____
    _____
    _____
    _____
    _____
    _____

2. Rebellion (Acts 5:29)

    I must obey God rather than men.

    a. Are you honest about your acts of open rebellion?

    b. If you know what God says is wrong, why do you continue to do the opposite of what He says?

    c. Are you allowing God's word to penetrate your heart?

d. Are you openly confessing your sin?

_____
_____
_____
_____
_____
_____
_____
_____
_____
_____
_____

3. Murder (Exodus 20:13)
    You shall not murder.
    a. Are you murdering people in your mind?
    b. Are you murdering in your heart?
    c. Are you murdering people in your conversation?

_____
_____
_____
_____
_____
_____

4. Intimidation (1 Samuel 18:29)

Then Saul was even more afraid of David. Thus, Saul was David's enemy continually.

    a.   Are you pushing past intimidation and staying the course the Lord has directed you to?

    b.   Are you giving room to the enemy in your life?

    c.   Do you believe that God is greater in you than the devil of this world?

5. Fear (Deuteronomy 31:8)

He will never leave you nor forsake you. Do not be afraid; do not be discouraged.' When you fear a situation or emotional challenge, really envision God saying this, just to you.

    a. Is fear hiding in your belly?

    b. Does fear control you?

    c. Are you using the authority given to you by God to command the fear in your life to flee?

6. Final Thoughts

LESSON 9

Overcomer

Overcomers are people who have stood through a process and allowed the Lord to bring them forth for the use of the Kingdom. God's Word says in 1 John 5:4, "For everyone born of God overcomes the world." This is the victory that has overcome the world, even our faith. That doesn't mean that there are not things that God still needs to correct. However, you are at a level that He can use you for His Kingdom. Just like when you first give your life to God, something falls off you at the altar. This is the same process when the Lord elevates you to service. As you teach others, God will show you what areas of your life that need to be healed, delivered, or trained. Service doesn't stop development. It speeds the process up. Maturity means you can handle correction on a faster and a heavier level. Thus, the Lord will call you. However, we are subject to the Lord on a greater level. God's Word says in James 3:1 (ESV), "Not many of you should become teachers, my brothers, for you know that we who teach will be judged with greater strictness." This statement is not a deterrence but caution to stay humble and allow those you teach to make room for growth as you grow. Never become high minded nor proud, for we know that haughty spirit comes before a fall. Thus, lest you fall, never forget where you come nor who called you to come. Everything is about Christ and nothing about us. You are merely a vessel in use for service.

STRONGHOLDS

1. Breakthrough (Matthew 16:18)
    The gates of hell shall not prevail against me.
    a. Are you ready for your breakthrough?
    b. Are you praising God for what He is about to do and has done in your life?

_____

_____

_____

_____

_____

_____

_____

_____

_____

_____

_____

_____

_____

2. Health Issues (Jeremiah 17:14)
    Heal me, O Lord, and I shall be healed; save me, and I shall be saved, for you are my praise.
    a. Do you believe God can heal you?
    b. Do you have the faith that God will heal you?

c. Do you trust God to heal you completely?

_____

_____

_____

_____

_____

_____

_____

_____

_____

_____

3. Cruelty (Genesis 1:27)

So, God created man in His own image, in the image of God, He created him; male and female He created them.

  a. Are you cruel to those who look different than you?

  b. Do you deny the unsaved the opportunity for God to move on their behalf by not praying for them?

_____

_____

_____

_____

_____

4. Nervous (1 Peter 5:7)
   Casting all your anxieties on him, because he cares for you.
   a. Are you giving God the issues of your heart?
   b. Do you trust the Lord with your whole heart, mind, and soul?

_____

5. Uncertainty (Romans 5:3)

I rejoice in my sufferings, knowing the suffering produces endurance.
a. Are you rushing your process of being made whole in Christ?
b. Are you rejoicing in the Lord during your troubles?

_____
_____
_____
_____
_____
_____
_____
_____
_____
_____

6. Final Thoughts:

_____
_____
_____
_____
_____

LESSON 10

Come Forth

The greater the call demands greater service, greater requirements, and more warfare. The Word of God speaks about different levels of callings. God's Word states in Acts 13:2, "While they were ministering to the Lord and fasting, the Holy Spirit said, "Set apart for me Barnabas and Saul for the work to which I have called them." God determines what office and level each believer is chosen for service. Some people are told the office in which they belong from their coverings in ministry. Some are told by other members of the body. Then it is those who hear directly from the Holy Spirit Himself. No matter if they try to deny what they heard or not, God will continue to pursue until they submit to the call or die. Many may feel unworthy, misunderstood, or even rejected by man. However, it doesn't excuse the fact that God called them.

Romans 8:28 states, "And we know that for those who love God all things work together for good, for those who are called according to His purpose." Many people see others going through a struggle, and they determine the worth of other people. Truly no man can determine the level or height God will use another man. As people of God, we need to learn to listen and wait for God's confirmation on our own and other lives to encourage and help them push past the warfare to accomplish the call on their lives. Remember, we are one body, but many members. Members of the body of Christ are for His use not for the glory unto man.

STRONGHOLDS

1. Liar (John 8:44)

You are of your father the devil, and your will is to do your father's desires. He was a murderer from the beginning, and has nothing to do with the truth, because there is no truth in him. When he lies, he speaks out of his own character, for he is a liar and the father of lies.
   a. Are you living a false life by not being true to yourself?
   b. Are you creating a fantasy life based on lies?

_____
_____
_____
_____
_____
_____
_____
_____
_____
_____
_____
_____

2. Lack (Psalm 34:10)

The young lions suffer want and hunger; but those who seek the Lord lack no good thing. I decree that I will no longer have lack in my life in the name of Jesus.

    a. Are you making your request unto the father in his presence?

    b. Do you believe that God will provide for you daily?

    c. Are you allowing God to provide for you? Do you satisfy your need based on your own desires?

_____
_____
_____
_____
_____
_____
_____
_____
_____
_____
_____

3. Battle (Psalms 27:1)

The LORD is my light and my salvation; whom shall I fear? The Lord is the defense of my life; whom shall I dread?

    a. Are you allowing the Lord to be your strength and joy while you're in the battle?

    b. Do you believe the false evidence that seems real presented by the devil?

c. Do you need God to deliver you from fear?

_____
_____
_____
_____
_____
_____
_____
_____
_____
_____
_____
_____

4. Revenge (1 Peter 3:9)

Do not repay evil for evil or reviling for reviling, but on the contrary, bless, for to this you were called, that you may obtain a blessing.

a. Are you looking for ways to pay those who wronged you back with evil?

b. Are you allowing God to heal your hurt?

c. Can you cast your pain on the Lord?

_____
_____
_____
_____
_____

5. Temptation (Matthew 26:41)

I will watch and pray that I may not enter into temptation. The spirit indeed is willing, but the flesh is weak.

    a.   Are you keeping your flesh under subjection by reading the Bible and spending time with the Lord?

    b.   Do you pray daily?

    c.   Do you sit quietly after prayer to wait for God to respond to your prayer?

6. Final Thoughts:-

LESSON 11

Words of Expression

This final chapter was created as an avenue for you to create words of expression that demonstrates to you the love of Your glorious Father in heaven. If you read the primary book that complements this workbook, you will see that Chapter 11 is my words of expression of the amazing power of Christ that healed my life. God loves to inhabit the praises of His people. Look at this writing as a love letter or poem of love to the Father for all that He has done for you.

1. Words of Expression:

_____
_____
_____
_____
_____
_____

Closing Remarks

The word of God says when God starts something, He brings it unto completion. Thus, I decree that as you study to show thy self-prove that the Lord will bring everything brought forth in your study will be brought to completion; complete healing and complete deliverance in Jesus' name. Amen.

About the Author

Zolisha L. Ware gave her life to Christ at the age of twenty-six just a few weeks short of her 27th birthday on August 28, 2004. Zolisha has been a member of Integrity Deliverance Ministry since that date. It wasn't long after giving her life did she received the gift of the Holy Ghost during the churches' 9th-anniversary service for Integrity Deliverance Ministry. Zolisha became the Praise & Worship Leader for the ministry in April 2005 where she has continued to hold that role still today. Sometime after being made the Praise & Worship Leader, she was also charged to lead the Dance Ministry within the church. Zolisha believes her most prized possession is her relationship unto the Lord. You can see the evidence within her singing and dancing unto the Lord.

Before a relationship with the Lord, Zolisha was robbed of her education by anger and bitterness due to the life struggles of being a teenage mother. However, once she became under the healing power of Jesus Christ, the Spirit of the Lord directed Zolisha in 2007 to pursue her education. Shortly after the ushering of the Spirit of the Lord to get her education, Zolisha found out that she should have already received her high school diploma. However, since it was so many years after that period, Zolisha was required to take two online tests. One which was an English examination and the other a Science examination to receive a fully accredited High School Diploma. I am glad to report she completed both tests online quickly. After completing the classes, Zolisha was awarded her High School diploma in September 2007 from Excel High School located in Plymouth, MN.

Once she was able to accomplish her high school diploma, she was continually driven by the Spirit of the Lord to further her education by signing up for college. Therefore, in the spring of 2008, Zolisha began to attend Lincoln College-Normal located. She received her Associates Degree in Arts in 2011, and three years later she received her Bachelors in Liberal Arts. Once Zolisha obtained her Bachelor's Degree, she thought she had completed her studies. However, the drive for education continued to burn heavily within her. Therefore, after consulting with the Lord, she enrolled in Liberty University located in Lynchburg, VA, in August of 2014. A year or so after being enrolled within the Master program in May of 2015, Zolisha encountered a supernatural dream that lasted for three nights. Within that dream, Zolisha was tested on things that the Lord had delivered her from like greed, anger, sexual immorality, hate, and perversion.

At the end of that dream, Zolisha was given a mandate straight from heaven to birth an outreach program geared toward helping women to be more Christ-centered. Thus, Safe Haven Women Outreach (SHWO) was birthed. Zolisha is the founder and President of the community outreach ministry and currently the program services in the Bloomington-Normal, IL Community area. Safe Haven Women Outreach also has an online presence, and you can find the outreach on Facebook by simply searching the name. Anyone regardless if they live in the Bloomington-Normal, IL Community or not can follow the page by simply liking the page. During Zolisha development of the outreach, she continued to pursue her education but at a slower pace while launching the outreach. SHWO's first day of service was April 16, 2016.

The program has been said to bring the deliverance power of God and transforms every life that steps within the thresholds of the outreach program. Once the program was fully up and running, Zolisha continued to pursue her education with Liberty University, where she received a Master's degree in Executive Leadership in March of 2017. Zolisha has stated that her education in the secular world has concluded and now has a mandate from heaven to learn all she can concerning the Kingdom of God. Zolisha believes that in God, learning never stops. She believes we all should be striving to have the mind of Christ by studying all we can to help us be more like Jesus. Therefore, her studies will continue until the Lord returns.

Contact Info:
Facebook//Instagram: Zolisha Ware
Email: infozlware@gmail.com
Facebook//Instagram: Safe Haven Women Outreach
Email: safehavenwomenoutreach@gmail.com

Works Cited

1. 2019 Merriam-Webster, I. (2019, April 5th). Identity Definition. Retrieved from Merriam-Webster: https://www.merriam-webster.com/dictionary/identity#synonyms
2. 2019 Merriam-Webster, I. (2019, May 29). Stronghold. Retrieved from Merriam Webster Dictionary: https://www.merriam-webster.com/dictionary/stronghold
3. Hub, 2. -2. (2019, March 31). Ephesians 6:4. Retrieved from Bible Hub: https://biblehub.com/ephesians/6-4.htm
4. Thompson, F. C. (2007). Thomas and Chain Study Bible. Indianapolis, IN: B.Bkirkbride Bible Co. INC.

www.ingramcontent.com/pod-product-compliance
Lightning Source LLC
Chambersburg PA
CBHW081729100526
44591CB00016B/2550